Advanced Secret Mind Control

Conversational Hypnosis and NLP

Learn the Secrets of Cult Leaders
and Master Manipulators!

William Horton, PsyD, CAC

ISBN:1500454664
ISBN-13:9781500454661

CONTENTS

INTRODUCTION

When you think of hypnosis, what do you think of? If you're like many people, you think of a person who talks in soothing tones to get a person to relax enough that they can be ushered into a sleep-like trance. Once there, the hypnotist can do various things to implant suggestions for the person to follow both in-trance and out-of-trance. Some stage hypnotists will even prompt their subjects to rather silly things to entertain the audience.

If those are some of the kinds of images that come to mind, I would now respectfully ask you to set those aside and come with me on a journey into a very different world – the world of *conversational hypnosis*

1

and *neuro-linguistic programming (NLP)*. They both involve communication with a person's unconscious mind, as does traditional hypnosis. The difference, however, is that the communication with the target's unconscious is achieved without using traditional deep-trance hypnotic states. In fact, it can be executed during the course of normal daily conversation.

Why would you want to use these techniques to communicate with another person's unconscious mind? The reason is simple: By using the techniques found in this book, your communication skills will greatly improve become much more effective in terms of exercising influence and getting people to do what you want them to do. This will put you on the pathway to a much happier and fulfilling life in which you not only have more influence on the people you encounter from day-to-day, you'll also have a great time doing it because the methods I teach are downright *fun* to use!

A quick word on semantics: I combine elements of both *conversational hypnosis* and *NLP* into my own unique approach, so to avoid repeating those phrases over and over, what you'll see throughout the book is CH/NLP.

Also, conversational hypnosis is often called *covert hypnosis*. I don't especially like that word because it carries with it, at least in my mind, a slight connotation of being "up to something," which to me is an unnecessarily manipulative approach.

The key to unlocking the power of secret mind control through CH/NLP is to realize the ubiquitous quality of *trance*. People go into trance all the time. In fact, the brain is often looking to escape into trance in many situations, and what we're doing with CH/NLP is facilitating that transition from normal waking consciousness to a waking hypnotic trance state. Once this transition is achieved, that is when you can exercise influence on the target to get them to do what you want them to do, and have them think that it was their idea all along! You can use these techniques just to have fun or to help people. For me, I have applied these techniques in my clinical practice to help people overcome such issues as uncontrolled anger, post-traumatic stress disorder (PTSD), obesity, smoking and many other situations that my clients wanted to change. Helping people change destructive behaviors is a very rewarding occupation.

How would your life be different if you could learn to use CH/NLP quickly and in everyday situations? The good news is that it really is quite easy to learn. Oddly enough, however, many traditional hypnotists and NLP practitioners don't actually understand CH/NLP the same way that I do. My unique approach is what allows me to teach others to easily and effortlessly use these techniques and methods for their benefit.

Complicating this picture is the fact that there are lots of what I call *unscrupulous pirates* who offer sham courses with little to no practical, useful information. It's an unfortunate situation, but one that should not be considered surprising. After all, lots of people want CH/NLP, which inevitably attracts some people to jump right in to try and fill that demand, whether they really know what they're doing or not! The problem is that all it takes is one bad experience with poorly executed training and people can get entirely turned off to CH/NLP. What I'm going to do is teach you a set of really useful skills that you can use in your daily life to improve your communication with and influence on others.

There are also people who do understand CH/NLP, but then they lack the necessary skills to teach it effectively. We've all experience poor teachers, haven't we? Being good at a skill doesn't automatically translate into to being a good teacher of that same skill. When a teacher isn't good at what they do, the end result is often making something much harder to learn that it really should be.

In the real world, many of the most famous people we know of use these techniques all the time. People like Barack Obama, Bill Clinton, Ronald Reagan, Adolf Hitler, Winston Churchill, Ghandi, even Martin Luther King. You'll notice that one of the things all of them hold in common is that they were and are great public speakers. Whether you agree with their actions or their rhetoric, they were all fantastically gifted speakers. They changed the world because of the power of their spoken words. And they all used basic hypnotic techniques – the same ones that I'm going to teach to you in this book. Mass marketing and advertising also makes very effective use of these methods, as do many of the best movies and stories.

To use these methods and techniques effectively, you have to first take the time to learn the fundamentals, the basics of the skill set. What happens a lot of times is that someone who has learned some traditional hypnosis skills tries to then take those into the conversational setting and use them. This simply doesn't work. The same thing applies with traditional NLP in the conversational setting. You end up trying to hard to be covert, and it ends up looking like you're trying to be slick. This can come off as being very condescending and manipulative – qualities that do not help you in your overall efforts at all.

Your own comfort is a key factor to highlight in this regard. If you're not comfortable with what you're trying to be, then your target's "BS radar" will pick right up on that. What I'm going to teach you is really not hard to do, but it does require more than just a few basic conversational techniques. You have to use frameworks and templates and scripts to get started, and many people don't like the idea of using those. However, if you stop and consider, you'll easily realize how important it is to utilize those items. It's like playing jazz music: There are a lot of fundamental skills you need to learn before you can just jump into a trio and start improvising. If you do that, you're pretty much guaranteed to fail, and look rather foolish in the process. Also, some people who learn CH/NLP fail to develop and *off switch*, which means they're just doing it all the time, which gets to be really tiresome for everyone.

What I'm going to do is teach you CH/NLP in just 4 simple steps:

1. Learn the easy way to do CH/NLP utilizing real world examples.

2. Change your mindset to one of having fun. If you make it into this huge effort that involves a lot of hard work, then you'll inevitably have trouble getting into it.

3. Follow a template that you can build upon and eventually make it your own.

4. Practice, practice, practice and find more real world examples of CH/NLP in action.

STEP 1: Realize that CH/NLP is very natural, which you

can easily see if you just look at real world examples. Politicians often become very good at these skills, especially during campaigns. Barack Obama, in his 2008 acceptance speech at the Democratic National Convention talked about how there will come a time in your life when a light will come down from above and you'll say to yourself, "I have to vote for Barack Obama." That simple part of his speech was packed full of CH/NLP techniques. There was the direct command *vote for Barack Obama*. The language about light coming down has various meanings. If you vote for him, you're in the light or enlightened, with the clear implication that if you don't vote for him, you must be in the dark. When you're in the voting booth, there will probably be light coming down from the ceiling, and it will trigger you to think about voting for him because he set up this whole scenario and the suggestion in your unconscious mind. Even his overall campaign themes of hope and change fall under these tecniques. Those are very hypnotic words, aren't they?

The key to your success is starting with baby steps. Build up your fundamentals first or you might fall on your face! Also remember that it's easier to start practicing this with strangers and clients rather than people who are close to you, which means don't start out trying this on your friends or family. They have too many preconceived notions about who you are, and if you start behaving differently from that, their "BS detector" is quickly activated. Strangers don't have those preconceived notions, offering you the opportunity to practice, to build your confidence in it, so that you can engage it comfortably with anyone.

I recommend that in general you should stay away from theory-heavy approaches that lack real-world examples. There's an old adage that applies to that kind of approach: *In theory it will work in practice, but in practice theory rarely works.* People who are always talking about research and theory without real world examples of it in action are the ones who can't really help you develop the real skills you need to build to be able to do this. I always teach this material with plenty of on-the-ground, real-world examples, which is what you need to excel.

STEP 2: Have fun with it! People are fascinating, so enjoy that and play with it. It won't always work, but those are sometimes your most valuable learning opportunities. There is no such thing as *failure*, there is only *feedback* that helps you get better and better. CH/NLP is powerful and will open doors for you. It will increase your traditional communication skills exponentially, allowing you to set up 90% of your work in advance. But you have to practice regularly, and also develop your "off switch."

STEP 3: Follow a template that you can start with and build upon from there. You can eventually improvise from that template, but you really need a solid starting point in the form of a script. This is a step-by-step process rooted in real world examples. Again, also play in safe zones and build out from there. Develop your confidence as you go.

STEP 4: Look for places in the real world where you're motivated to do things differently, learn how to decode those situations, then start small and build up from there. Bill Clinton won the presidency by learning basic anchoring techniques and eliciting strong emotional responses and then anchoring those to himself. Obama is another great example. Many people said he should wait before running, but he had a blank slate because he was essentially unknown, and it's always easier to paint on a blank slate. He used hypnotic words that worked so well because people didn't have a lot of preconceived notions about him as a person. He had a template and he followed it. So you can look at people who do it and learn from them.

Here's an example: When I'm talking to someone, I'll often ask them a few questions about color. "What's your favorite color? RED. Great. What color means peace and tranquility to you. BLUE. Great. What color means power and focus to you? RED." From just those few interactions, I learned some really important information that will facilitate my CH/NLP with that person. That person is a "power person" and will respond more to power techniques like direct commands and suggestions. And then I can take them into the tranquil place as well, building on blue when I need that. It just opens up the possibilities and opportunities. These kinds of insights into people are really important. If the person had said TEAL, that's more towards the blue spectrum than red, giving a clue on where to start with them. I might also ask them how old they were when they learned to drive, which immediately puts them into an age regression that they have to think about. "Did you learn on a stick or automatic?" I'm watching their eyes as they do this, to see if can they answer quickly or if they have to take time with it. What they do with their eyes lets me know if they're kinesthetically-oriented or auditory-oriented or mentally-oriented. There are all sorts of seemingly innocent questions to ask that help you later in your interactions with people.

My approach is tried and true because I've been *doing* it for 30 years and *teaching* it for 25 years. You can learn this as well by spending as little as about 55 minutes each week on it. Each chapter of this book will end with a series of what I called *Challenges*. I don't like to call it homework because for many people there is a negative connotation to the idea of homework. I keep these challenges rooted in real-world examples and always encourage you to see what is fun in doing them. And now you are ready to rise to the challenge of learning CH/NLP!

1 JUMPSTART YOUR SKILLS

Many people who have heard about CH/NLP have preconceived notions about what it is or their ability to learn it. What are your own ideas and beliefs about CH/NL? In my many years of experience, here are some of the preconceived ideas and beliefs I've heard from people:

Hard to do

Tricky

Manipulative

Underhanded

Lots of rules

Sometimes people even think that because they know a bit about it that everyone must already know about it, right? Nothing could be further from the truth! Most people really don't have any idea how CH/NLP works or the many benefits it can bring to their lives. It's a set of skills that just about anyone can learn. In fact, some of you are already doing it without even being aware that you're doing it! But as soon as hear the word *skill*, we often assume it must be something hard to learn. Part of what this book is meant to do is debunk that myth.

I also want to reiterate that there many the teachers who make it seem harder than it is because their true motive is making sure they seem smarter than everyone else. Those are the teachers and trainers that come off as condescending. They make it sound like they are smarter than the audience and smarter than other trainers. They set an artificially high bar as a way of limiting other people getting into it rather than really sharing. That is what I consider to be the epitome of manipulative behavior!

Then there's a real lack of knowledge on some of the basic rules of hypnosis and how the mind works, and often an assumption that conversational CH/NLP and traditional hypnosis somehow operate by different rules, but they don't. They do the same thing, but they do use different methods. In fact, I would venture that the principles are often are easier to apply in the conversational setting than nearly any other setting.

Now that you've had a chance to identify your own beliefs, opinions and preconceived notions about CH/NLP, I want you to consider these further question: Where do you think those beliefs and opinion came from? How did you develop them? Did you have a previous bad experience with someone who claimed to be an expert? Did you read a book about it that was confusing and made it seem really hard?

Whatever the source of your ideas and beliefs about CH/NLP might be, if your current preconceived notions are holding you back from deeply engaging with these concepts and mastering them, then what you really have to do is *change* those beliefs in order to fully engage in the process and learn the skills. You won't be able to master these skills without changing any beliefs that are blocking or impeding your progress.

This is when it is helpful to think about and name what beliefs would you like to have, that might be more useful as you begin this journey with me into the world of CH/NLP. Here are some examples you might try on:

> The skills are natural and easy – you're already doing much of it.

> It's FUN to play with people using these methods and techniques.

> Going from traditional forms of hypnosis and NLP to CH/NLP is a natural transition.

> A solid foundation in traditional approaches will make switching to CH/NLP easier.

As you can easily see, you can flip the wrong-headed, unproductive beliefs and turn them into much more positive ones. You're letting go of the old beliefs and replacing them with new ones that work better. I always advise people to take what works and leave the rest!

I learned to do that through two of my main hobbies: Theatre and the martial arts. Bruce Lee is the probably the best-known icon of the martial arts, and he radically changed them. He would first learn the basic rules and traditional approaches, but after mastering them he would then proceed to break them and do all kinds of new, innovative moves that he invented for himself. You have to learn the fundamentals of the tradition so that you can then go on to make it your own by breaking the rules. Keep what works for *you* and throw out the rest. There are specific styles of martial arts that will work well for you if your build is of a certain type, but if you aren't that type, then you have to find a different way or approach to make it work for you.

I also love taking theatre and acting classes. Sometimes you just need to be reminded of what you already know, especially if you haven't been practicing lately. In acting, what are the rules? Really, it ends up being *whatever works for you*, just like in the martial arts world. I have to learn to play to my strengths in both the martial arts and in the theatre based on who I am, my type, my build, and so on. Take what works and leave the rest. That's how you flip your beliefs.

One of the most basic hypnotic techniques that applies

to the conversational setting is *split consciousness*.
Splitting a person's attention or consciousness causes
them to go into a trance, and that is where the belief
flipping can occur more easily. Here's a quick example
of how it can work in this specific context: As you think
about the rules or beliefs that are impeding you, look at
your hands. Now look at back again to this page of the
book but still pay attention to your hands, and you'll
notice your hands – how they feel, and how one feels
different and draws your attention. Maybe it's your
dominant hand, but maybe it isn't. But what you notice
is a slight tingling sensation in that hand, and isn't that
interesting? And then you can also realize how your
mind is tuned in to all sorts of things just under your
awareness. Like the place where you live. You used to
live someplace else, but now you live where you live.
It's not good or bad, it just is. Where you used to live
just isn't relevant anymore. Now take that tingling hand
and realize that all the limiting beliefs you have about
CH/NLP are in that tingling hand. Now you can easily
realize that it's tingling because you're ready to let go of
all those limiting beliefs about CH/NLP that are in that
hand. Your other hand isn't tingling because it has the

beliefs you want to hang on to. The calm and cool hand is the one that wants to grasp these concepts and move forward, to make the change of putting in the beliefs that are good for you now. You realize that you can do CH/NLP and put that into your present mind, just like you know where you live now. And take those limiting beliefs and put them into the part of your mind that knows you used to live someplace else but that just isn't relevant to you anymore.

That was just a very quick script that used some rules of normal hypnosis in a very conversational way. The split consciousness occurs when you ask a person to look at one thing but pay attention to another thing.

You've probably heard that the conscious mind is just 10% of our brain that we use for analysis, rational thought, logic, short-term memory and willpower. But that's only the virtual tip of the iceberg. This iceberg concept is important to grasp. The Titanic was sunk by what was *under* the water's surface – the 90% of the iceberg that no one could see. I believe it was Albert Einstein who gave us the notion that we typically only use about 10% of our mind's capacity. We think we're rational, but we're really not. We use our rational minds to rationalize things, like the smoker I met who just couldn't seem to quit. He had recently changed jobs and was now making less money than he used to make, and he was very stressed out about that and the new job wasn't much to his liking. He claimed to be too stressed out to quit. But then why is he spending all that money on smoking? It's simply not logical. It's not rational, because none of us are really rational!

In hypnosis, what we have to do is bypass the 10% to get to the 90% that 90% is the home of habits, emotions, long-term memory, beliefs, values and emotions. In CH/NLP we use the 10% to leverage ourselves into the 90% of the mind where we can really accomplish things. We have to bypass the *Critical Factor of the mind*, the barrier that prevents things from getting down into the deeply-held stuff that is carefully guarded and protected. The Critical Factor is what stands in the way, causing things to be rejected with emotion.

Traditional hypnosis uses *permission* and *relaxation* to bypass the Critical Factor. It's based on *compounding* and *repetition*. Once relaxed, the Critical Factor falls aside, which paves the way for using compounding and repetition of the suggestion in all sorts of different ways to get it planted firmly way down there in the 90% portion of the mind.

CH/NLP uses *structure* to disarm the Critical Factor and other techniques that don't challenge. Thinking back to the brief example about splitting attention, there was nothing challenging about it, but it encouraged you to just *realize* what was happening. CH/NLP uses *naturally occurring states* to bypass the Critical Factor. You don't challenge, you just take a structural approach in looking at both the belief and the rational part in a way that induces trance, which occurs naturally when you set up a conflict between the conscious and subconscious. By bypassing the Critical Factor, we can induce change at the subconscious level, which will then automatically be rationalized by the conscious mind. Neurosis occurs when such conflicts exist over time without adequate resolution.

However, if you get too caught up in the techniques of CH/NLP, you lose **rapport**. Rapport is the key to successful CH/NLP. If you lose rapport, you will come across as manipulative and condescending. Get and maintain rapport, otherwise you shutdown the feedback loop you're trying to keep open and to influence. Rapport is essentially that feeling of flow or being in synch with the person you're talking to. You know when you have it because the conversation just feels very natural and easy-going, like the concept of "being on the same page." You achieve rapport by such basic techniques as *mirroring* **and** *matching*, and by picking up on the target's **VAK Preference** (visual, auditory, kinesthetic), which means how they prefer to take in or learn new information. The sooner you find that out, the better you can engage in the kind of mirroring and matching that leads to excellent rapport. You just have to really tune in to the other person, pick up on the cues, and then use that information moving forward. Mirroring and matching involves just what it sounds like — you pay attention to the patterns the other person shows in how they speak, faces they make, gestures and posture, and you mimic those as well. The basic idea is that a person trusts you quicker if you seem more like them than different from them.

Obviously, you must engage mirroring and matching in a non-obvious way in order to avoid triggering the other person's "BS detector."

A great summary of the characteristics of people who lean towards one element of VAK learning than another is provided by Just in Time Learning, and reviewing this material will help you pick up on the cues your target gives you about their VAK preference, or will give you ideas about what subtle questions you can ask to find out. Here's the run-down:

Visual learning style involves the use of seen or observed things, including pictures, diagrams, demonstrations, displays, handouts, films, flip-chart, etc. People with a visual VAK preference are neat and orderly; speak quickly; are good long-range planners and organizers; are observant and notice details; remember faces (but maybe not names); are appearance-oriented in both dress and presentation; are good spellers and can actually see the words in their minds; remember what was seen, rather than heard; memorize by visual association; like to read; can't remember jokes; like to write and draw pictures; have good handwriting; usually are not distracted by noise; might forget verbal instructions unless they're written down; are strong, fast readers; would rather read than be read to.

Auditory learning style involves the transfer of information through listening: Through speech sounds and noises. People with an auditory preference tend to speak in rhythmic patterns; talk to themselves while occupied; are easily distracted by noise; might move their lips and pronounce the words as they read; enjoy reading aloud and listening to others reading; like to hear someone explain something, and explaining things to other people; can repeat back and mimic tone pitch and timbre; find writing difficult, and are better at telling; are frequently eloquent speakers; are talkative, love discussion, and go into lengthy descriptions; have problems with projects that involve visualization, such as cutting pieces that fit together; can spell better out loud than in writing; like music more than art; Outgoing personality.

Kinesthetic learning involves physical experience – touching, feeling, holding, doing, practical hands-on experiences. People with a kinesthetic preference learn by doing; speak slowly; use action words; touch people to get their attention; stand close when talking to someone; are physically oriented and move a lot; wear clothes for comfort; like to make things; memorize by walking and seeing; might not enjoy reading; might use a finger as a pointer when reading; respond to physical rewards; willing to try new things; wave their hands when talking, i.e. use gestures a lot; can't sit still for long periods of time; tap a pencil or their foot while studying; can't remember geography unless they've actually been there; like plot-oriented books; reflect action with body movement as they read, and might walk around while reading.

It's also worth noting that many people have multiple VAK styles that they use, but will usually display a preference for one above the others. Just keep in mind that it's not a completely black-and-white distinction with many people.

Another key concept is that you have to be *willing to enter the trance state yourself* along with the other person. You basically have to do this in order to maintain the rapport that is required for successful CH/NLP.

Getting to and maintaining rapport can be difficult if someone has strongly held beliefs that run counter to your own. You have to learn to set aside your own beliefs and opinions in those situations in order to achieve true rapport – which can be easier said than done! As you achieve rapport, the target will naturally begin revealing even more information that you can use to trigger a trance state. What you're paying attention to now are words that elicit strong attachment or emotion from the target. These powerful words are ones that I call **Magic Personal Trance Words** (MPTWs) because they work like magic once you have identified them. What they do is serve as an inroad to bypass the Critical Factor and get you to the subconscious mind of the target.

The mind actually wants to escape into trance in order to avoid any kind of overload, such as occurs when you use the *split consciousness* technique mentioned earlier. It's a kind of defense mechanism. The mind is always on the lookout for existential threats, which comes from our early days as a species when we were both predators *and* prey. The brain has a deeply embedded skill of doing that. When you get a person to do the hard work of doing both things (looking at one thing but paying attention to another), the result will be going into the trance state. A musician who's really into their playing is doing something (playing the instrument), but their mind is elsewhere. The same thing happens in sports. It's what people call being in "the zone." You're doing the thing that you're doing, but your mind might be elsewhere. These are naturally occurring trance states.

In order to discover a person's MPTWs, you have to achieve a certain level of rapport in order for those to come out and be revealed. They are words that are emotionally charged in a way that begins to melt any resistance a person may be feeling towards you. They open up the target's mind to let you in. Never challenge MPTWs, just use them to get to where you're trying to go. If you challenge them, the target will immediately resist, rapport will be stifled and getting a trance state will be next to impossible. For example, I was having a conversation with a client, a veteran, who was having anger issues after a brain injury and was especially behaving poorly towards female nurses at the clinic. As I spoke with him, MPTWs were popping up all over the place – words like respect, honor, duty, and commitment. Using those words got him very quickly into trance where I could lead him through all kinds of suggestions and visualizations that would trigger him to think about relaxed, peaceful settings that helped him get his anger and inappropriate behaviors under control. You tap into the targets own beliefs and strongly held opinions through the MPTWs in order to plant suggestions for behavior change. And it works!

Chapter 1 Challenges:

Watch Fox News to tune into what MPTWs are being used.

Watch MSNBC for the same.

Watch some Darren Brown YouTube videos for the same .

Pick a stranger to start a conversation with and use your rapport skills to elicit MPTWs.

Do Split Consciousness using the target's own MPTWs.

Repeat 3 times.

Have fun!

Remind yourself that *this is easy!*

2 BUILD YOUR CONFIDENCE

I want to begin this chapter by asking you how your work on the challenges went. Did you have any problems with them? Some people have a hard time setting aside their personal beliefs to really engage. For example, if you're a strong liberal, just tuning in to Fox News can be quite a difficult thing to do! But it's important to practice this setting aside of your own beliefs and opinions in order to achieve the rapport necessary for successful CH/NLP.

There are many ways to bypass the Critical Factors of the mind. I've already introduced you to building rapport using mirroring/matching and tuning in to VAK preferences in your target. I've also mentioned the importance of MPTWs (Magic Personal Trance Words) in this process as well. Other methods and techniques include *Stacked Realities*, *Metaphors* and *Storytelling*, *Time Loops*, *Disjointed Logic*, *Implied Trance* and *Logical Levels*. Each of these will come up and be dealt with fully in subsequent chapters of this book.

One concept that will help you achieve that all-important rapport you need with your target is **Signal Recognition Technique** (or Technology). The goal here is to go beyond the basic mirroring/matching and VAK preference recognition to actually fully align your energy with that of your target. You essentially want to be recognized by your target as someone that can be trusted, someone that they are already very close to even when in reality they don't know you at all. There's a visualization aspect to this that is very important to execute, even if you think it sounds silly.

Begin by visualizing yourself in a conversation with someone you're very close to. There's a bubble of energy around you and there's a bubble of energy around that person that you're very close to, that you know really well and that you always slip into easy rapport with. As you slip into the comfortable state of rapport with that person, imagine that your bubble of energy extends outward, as does theirs, and that the two bubbles of energy intermingle and become one. You can read that person you know so well because your energy is in alignment with their own energy. Now, the next time you want to engage in CH/NLP with a stranger, from the first moment visualize your energy intermingling with the target's energy just like it does when you're having a nice easy conversation with that other person you are so close to. Anchor this image of unifying energies in yourself and consciously project that image when you go to interact with a stranger. When you meet a stranger, you want a very open and affirming kind of energy to be projecting from you. You see, that other person is going to be trying to figure out where to "put" you in their own mind, and if the energy you're sending to them is one that is the same as you send to person you know really well, then they will automatically put you in that place in their own mind. It makes achieving rapport so much easier if you have this frame of mind at the outset!

Something that will help you trigger this when you go to

interact with someone is to anchor it to yourself with an actual word or phrase – something you can say or whisper to yourself as you're about to interact with someone. I use a lot of military analogies and terms, if you haven't already noticed, because that's just what works for me, so the phrase I use is *target acquisition*. I also combine this with one or several physical gestures that help trigger the state. I might tilt my head slightly to one side in a kind of fun way, smile a nice smile and rub my hands together as I say the phrase in my head. I might even do a quick "eyebrow flash" which sends a signal as if to say, "Oh, I know this person!" With a good triggering routine like that, you'll be able to drop into that state and send just the right energy to jumpstart good rapport with whoever you're dealing with.

At the same time, develop your off-switch routine as well, because there's nothing more annoying to everyone than someone who just can't disengage the CH/NLP process. If you can't turn it off, you'll inevitably come across as always "on the make" or being manipulative. For me, it's a very simple sighing exhalation with a simultaneous dropping of my hands down to my sides. You know that people in the helping industries (doctors, psychologists, social workers) have to be able to develop an off-switch as well. If they don't, then they wind up never letting go of their work, which eventually hampers their ability to help anyone at all, so please take the time to develop your own off-switch. Everyone needs down-time where they're not engaging these methods and techniques.

After you get used to using rapport, MPTWs and Split Consciousness, you'll easily realize how you can lead people into whatever mental states you desire. The sky's the limit, really, whether it's doubt, confidence, fear, excitement, power, motivation, confusion and so on.

You may be wondering why you would ever want to lead anyone towards doubt and confusion. Well, haven't you come across people who are just too sure about what they *think* know? As a teacher and trainer, I come across this all the time, and sometimes it's useful to lead someone towards doubt and confusion in order to get them questioning their assumptions and realizing that maybe they don't know everything they think they know! A hint of fear (just a hint) is useful in helping people follow your commands – they need to slightly fear the consequences of not following your lead! Then again, when it comes to athletes engaged in highly competitive sports, you might want to lead them more towards fearlessness in order to get out there and play their best (and the best coaches are very good at this). Victims of abuse may need a boost in sensing their own innate power and control. A weight-loss client might need a boost in motivation to attend the next session or achieve the next milestone in their weight loss journey. In all these cases, what you're doing is actively changing their state of consciousness on the fly to get them to go where you want them to go.

Speaking of confusion, a great way to utilize it to induce trance in a target is through the concept of *Stacked Realities*. This is a very simple process that happens all the time in the real world. You very consciously set up a situation verbally in which the target will naturally get lost in confusion, which then triggers the brain to want to escape *into* trance. Once the state of confusion sends them into trance, then you have the option to take them to a whole new state of consciousness that is more useful for your intended purposes. The easiest way to do this is to tell a story that has too many layers or references within it for the person to sort out as you're saying it. I often use a series of people references, but you can also use a series of place references. This will be much more powerful if you have already elicited some of the target's MPTWs and can put them into the mix as well. For example, I was conversing with a fellow who revealed a number of MPTWs such as integrity, caring and trust. So I already had a certain level of rapport going which allowed those to be revealed. When I'm ready to induce trance in this target, I might say something like this: "I can understand that, because life really is all about caring with integrity. That reminds me of a story that my cousin told me about this guy he knew whose uncle was working for a friend to try and straighten out his accounting books which had gotten messed up by a previous employee who he trusted but who lacked integrity and was embezzling money from the business..." Even just after this one sentence, the level of confusion had the target's eyes glazing over, dropping his arms and tilting his head to one side, clear indications that his brain was confused enough to start slipping into trance.

A similar technique is making use of **Disjointed Logic**. This is especially effective when you're dealing with a very anal type of personality in a target. You begin by using general logic that they can agree with in order to build a nice rapport, but then in small steps you start introducing bits of logic that don't quite line up but aren't enough to trigger the good old "BS detector." It's actually fun to see how far down a particular rabbit hole you can lead someone with this technique. Eventually, you'll hit such an extremely disjointed form of logic that the person will literally snap out of trance in anger at what you're saying. This kind of technique is not one you can typically do in the course of just one short conversation. In fact, some of the most effective examples of it are ones that occurred over *years*, such as Hitler's clearly disjointed logic that lead so many Germans to want to exterminate the Jewish people. There's simply no quick logical way to persuade people to do something like that, but bit-by-bit over many years he got away with some extremely disjointed logic that people continued to buy into.

Now is also a good time to begin introducing you to the kinds of **Hypnotic Language Patterns** that will greatly aid all of your CH/NLP efforts. There are distinct patterns of speech that help induce and maintain trance and implant suggestions. I'm going to introduce you to 10 right now, and then 10 more in the next chapter and so on until I've shared all 50 of the with you that I have developed over the years. Here are the first 10:

1. I'm wondering if...

I'm wondering if you will, right now, while you have the opportunity, go ahead and make an appointment for a hypnosis session. I'm wondering if knowing that you can get the relief that you want from stress by the use of hypnosis will give you a feeling of security. I'm wondering if you can imagine being totally smoke-free and know the good feelings that will give you. I'm wondering if a man in your position would need follow up sessions for other things. *[I never told you to do anything. I was just wondering....]*

2. Maybe you'll...

Maybe you'll direct some unusual embedded

commands to your prospects while you are convincing them to use your services. Maybe you'll dream of other reasons for being hypnotized. Maybe you'll even spot the embedded commands in these sentences.

3. You probably already know...

You probably already know that most people who try it are helped by hypnosis. You probably already know that hypnosis is being used by more and more people every day. *[And what do you do in response to this statement? You might begin to think of reasons that I say you know for being hypnotized and of course you are likely to find them if you think long enough. If I wanted you to really search for these answers I probably could say: On a deep level, you probably already know how useful indirect communication can be]*

4. Don't _____ too quickly.

[This phrase has the implication that what I suggest will definitely happen anyway, and all I really care about is when it happens. And, if you are resisting me, your internal response may well be: "Oh yeah, who says I can't do this quickly! I'll show you!" Isn't that great?]

Don't decide to be hypnotized too quickly. Don't begin thinking about how much better you will look and feel when you are at your ideal weight before you've even been hypnotized. Don't begin having too much fun with these language patterns too quickly or too soon.

5. Can you imagine...

[You probably already know that people are more likely to do what they are familiar with and that imagining something is a great way to create familiarity] Can you imagine how much better you will feel when you are smoke-free? Can you imagine how much money you could save from being smoke-free? Can you imagine all the situations where you would use this language pattern if you practiced it and really knew it? Can you imagine the power of just this one language pattern?

6. One can, <person's name>, _____

[By adding the person's name at the beginning of the embedded command, you will make it much more powerful] One can, Bill, feel good about having the kind of help that hypnosis gives you. One can, Barbara, enjoy the thrill of being at your ideal weight.

7. You might notice the feelings... as you...

You might notice the feelings of excitement you experience as you consider the rewards of being stress-free. You might notice the feelings of satisfaction as you provide another opportunity for an indirect suggestion. You might notice the feelings of happiness that you have as you contemplate how good you look at your ideal weight.

8. A person might, <person's name>, _____

[Say the person's name close to the second half of the sentence, and it becomes a personal embedded command] A person might, Sarah, take the lessons from that situation and realize how valuable it would be to experience hypnosis for yourself. A person might, Allen, find some good reasons that would make being hypnotized compelling.

9. One Could _____, because...

[Because is the magic word, because it lends emotional credibility to whatever goes before it] Once could use the word "because" after important suggestions, because you enjoy trying new things. One could let this

learning go to a very deep place inside, because you may not be completely aware of how important it is yet. One could experience hypnosis because that person was completely aware of how important it is to be smoke free. One could desire to be self-assured, because one knows how important that can be in dealing with others.

10. You can _____, because...

[Here's that because word again] You can just use it and discover how powerful it is, because you can pretty much say anything you want after it. You can believe it works, because it is such a nice way to keep talking and keep the suggestions coming. You can even use it in everyday conversations, because people love to hear reasons for things. You can experience hypnosis now, Stanley, because you want to be the very best you can be, don't you?

Chapter 2 Challenges:

Practice obtaining good rapport.

Engage your SRT.

Use your off-switch.

Try the MPTWs and Spilt Consciousness with new targets.

Do 3 Stacked Realities that take a target to a new state.

If applicable, do a Disjointed Logic routine.

Practice the Hypnotic Language Patterns daily.

Have Fun!

3 A REAL-WORLD TEMPLATE

One question that often comes up with beginners related to CH/NLP is this: How do you keep yourself from going into trance? The answer to this question is simple: You don't! Recall that in Chapter 1 (Jumpstart Your Skills) I made the point that you do in fact have to be willing to enter the trance state yourself. It's the only way to maintain the rapport that is essential to these techniques. Only by entering the trance state yourself can you maintain rapport and have the opportunity to lead targets where you want them to go. I think the confusion about this comes from the fact that in CH/NLP the trance state we're talking about is a *waking* trance state, which is why it's often also called *waking hypnosis*. The trance is not so deep as to simulate the sleep-like trance of traditional hypnosis. You're conscious the whole time. So again, you *must* enter the trance state yourself. Don't resist it; go with it! You will yourself have a split consciousness happening, with one part of you in trance and the other part consciously guiding the interactions and the target in the direction you want to take.

Also keep in mind that if you feel like you're having trouble finding a person's MPTWs in social situations, then most likely you're *trying too hard*, which means you're really making it harder than it needs to be. You can get there much quicker if you talk about divisive issues, but then you have to be really good at setting aside your own beliefs. You just have to start asking the kinds of questions that will elicit the target's MPTWs, as was discussed earlier in some of the examples I gave.

In this chapter I'm going to share some essential information about *Time Loops* and *Implied Trance*. Both use naturally occurring events and states in life to trigger the trance state, and they can also be used together in a highly complementary way.

Time Loops refer to particular times of day when it's

much easier to get people to go into trance because their minds and bodies are already primed for it. Almost without any prompting at all, these are times of day when people are prone to just "spacing out," which means they're naturally on the edge of the trance state to begin with. These times of day or particular events can include the following:

Mid-afternoon

End of business day

Late evening

After stressful event

The Mid-Day Crash: You know that feeling you get in the middle of the afternoon, after lunch, when both your blood sugar and dopamine levels just seem to drop off precipitously. If you work in an office, this is often your toughest time of day, where it feels nearly impossible to concentrate and focus on the work you know you should be doing. This is a time of day when people very naturally want to and often do just slip into an alter state. To complete the transition into trance for the target, you need to do very little, so this is one time when shorter is better as far as what you do. By building on this natural cycle of the day, you might not need to do much more than say something like, "Your eyes are feeling heavy," and the target goes right into trance. This is an ideal time for CH/NLP as well as traditional hypnosis because of how close the person is to trance to begin with.

End of the Business Day: This is another time that is absolutely prime for people going into trance. When people get to the end of their business day, they just automatically mentally check out. That's when it's useful to go after that time such as at a conference, when the time comes for the end of the day's conference activities, people are already mentally checking out, so then you can lead them right into what you want them to do. A very short script in this type of situation could run as follows:

> "You might be kind of checking out, thinking
> about what you're going to eat for dinner.
> Now think how good that's going to be, and
> really, it's just like how good it feels to be in
> this session and learning this valuable

information that you're learning."

Their minds are going elsewhere, so you're just going to guide them out and back. Physicians could really use this to get people to follow post-treatment maintenance plans and so forth. The doctors could implant where they want patients to put their prescription bottles, such as, "Put it by your toothbrush if you have to take the medication in the morning."

Evening: This is such a good time to go for the trance state. People are already sleepy or tired. If they've also been overwhelmed by their day, then the mind literally wants to escape into trance. Throughout history people have used this time of day to trigger the trance state by making use of storytelling. Stories told around the campfire at night, reading books to children near bedtime, and for many people in modern times, winding down by watching television. In the evening, these are all activities that very easily induce trance in targets. Speaking of television, advertisers are very well aware of making use of this prime trance time. The interrupting of the program being watched with commercial breaks sets up an automatic split consciousness situation that the advertiser can then use to implant suggestions about buying their products. In your own scripts that you use at this time of day, you want to anchor as much of it as possible to the metaphor of "later" or "late" to more easily get the target to shift into the trance state.

Stressful Events: During or immediately following stressful events is another prime time for inducing the trance state. This is why first responders to the scene of an accident or disaster often have to shout at people to break the trance state they've already slipped into in order to get them to follow simple directions. You can also create stress and then use the stress you've created in the target to shift people into trance. All you really have to do is start talking in a way that really makes a person uncomfortable. As they begin to show signs of the stress state, that's your cue to engage in methods that will gently lead them right into trance. It's a natural stress/trance response that is very useful to keep in mind.

For example, once when I was teaching a class, there was a young lady who came in rather late. I wanted to get a point across to her that being late was not okay, but I could use this as prime example of showing how to create stress that leads to trance. So I really lit into her, criticizing her for thinking that she was so much more important than everyone else that she didn't need to get to class on time and how disrespectful that was not only to me as the teacher but to all her fellow students, who she would then have to rely upon to get the information that she had missed by being late. I mean I really let her have it in a way that had the entire class feeling really uncomfortable and stressed out about my reaction. Then I just said, "Okay, let's get back on track here. Everyone close your eyes and take a couple of nice deep breaths." They were all so stressed out and uncomfortable that they totally wanted to escape into trance, and that was all I had to do to get them all into that state. If you're ever teaching a class and there's a fire drill, once you're all back in class and getting settled, it's an ideal time to use that same short script and you'll probably get the entire class into a trance state in one fell swoop.

High Emotional States: These very easily bypass the critical factors of the mind, although they are not as dramatic/traumatic as stress, but they still operate in much the same way. Because they're not quite as powerful as the stressful events, your script might have to be a little more involved or longer, but you can still leverage those times of high emotion to induce trance.

Keep in mind that the more knowledge you have of your target, the easier all of these moments become for leveraging time loops and events into the trance state. Knowing your targets' MPTWs makes it even easier, so make sure you're constantly on the lookout for finding those or eliciting them from your targets.

Here's another classroom example. If you're a teacher and you're teaching, you should have people introduce themselves, and what you do is pay close attention to what people are saying because they're going to be giving you PTWs. If it's mid-afternoon, you can get them to go into trance really easily with a simple confusion technique, which is something that many teachers excel at without even trying very hard! In the therapy setting, that first get-to-know-the-client session is another very useful time in asking guiding questions that will naturally lead to the target revealing the MPTWs – all you have to do is pay close enough attention to recognize them when they come out. All of this also applies in other settings, whether its seduction or sales that you're working on – use these events, questions and time loops to lead the target where you want them to be.

Implied Trance is another useful concept. You set this up by asking the target what their beliefs are about trance (or hypnosis or altered states). It doesn't really matter what they actually are because you're going to use whatever they give you. This is a leverage moment, not a teaching moment. You don't want to try to teach them a different kind of belief or opinion, but you're going to leverage whatever their belief is that they've given you. You're essentially using a lot of words that are about trance and altered states to imply that the target is already there or heading there, and because the target is focused on the words you're saying, they're not really questioning the truth of what you're saying, which means they subconsciously accepting the the trance state that has already been implied.

Be careful to **never take away the mystery and magic**

of it these processes. In fact, you want to blow that up to be even larger than it might already be. Make it bigger, because people reall do love magic and mystery. Never ever say it's just like "relaxation" because there's only one response that ever elicits, which is this: "Oh, then why bother? So what?" Have you ever noticed that biggest, longest-running and most successful acts in Las Vegas are almost always magicians? Everyone wants to be entertained with mystery and magic.

Another thing to keep in mind that you can **use the target's intellect against them**. For example, let's say your target thinks of themselves as very intelligent or intellectual. You can easily leverage that to your advantage. You can bolster that belief of the target by giving them a takeaway such as, "Only lower-intelligent, less-educated people have problems with trance." What these leverage points are all meant to do is to free up the subconscious mind.

Leverage fear: You can easily see how fear is a great motivator, right? And yet people *want* to be afraid, especially in a controlled environment where they know it will end without any real harm coming to them. Think about people who are thrill-seekers, or how many people like to see horror movies. Why is that? The answer is surprisingly simple: When the stress is released, it feels really good! So blow up the fear factor and leverage that into implying and then inducing the trance state in your targets. The more extreme the examples, in this case, the better, because that increases the leverage power of what you're doing.

If you're having a really tough time with a target, then it's time for a *reality check*. Some people really just aren't worth the effort it takes to get them into trance. Learn to recognize when that is happening and just stop trying. In my experience, control freaks are too much work to bother with. They are a real challenge, yes, and I also believe it's simply not worth the effort. The same thing applies with the pirates who just want to steal what you have (your power). Then there are also the small-minded people who just can't break out of their tiny boxes. And people who are just jerks in a general sense. Don't waste your time on people who really don't want to get into these processes, who aren't interested. It's a waste of your valuable time and effort.

It is also critical to pay attention to **after-trance moments**. Many practitioners and trainers often miss these key opportunities. After any kind of formal trance event, the person will be conpletely wide open to all kinds of suggestions because they *think* they're not in trance any more, but they really still are in trance on some level, and you can leverage that as well. Different kinds of post-trance moments, including natural trances, such as after a movie, just before sleeping, just after waking up, or after sex are times when people become prime targets for post-trance suggestions. When children first wake up in the morning is an awesome time to plant super-positive messages into their brains, or for your partner as well. In sports, during the game, athletes are in the "zone," which is an altered trance state, so right *after* the game, they're wide open for all kinds of good, positive suggestions, and it doesn't matter if they had won or lost the game just played.

Below are more hypnotic language patterns for you to become familiar with:

6. One can, <person's name>, _____

[By adding the person's name at the beginning of the

embedded command, you will make it much more powerful.] One can, Bill, feel good about having the kind of help that hypnosis gives you. One can, Barbara, enjoy the thrill of being at your ideal weight. *[Who can? One can.]*

7. You might notice the feelings... as you...

You might notice the feelings of excitement you experience as you consider the rewards of being stress-free. You might notice the feelings of satisfaction as you provide another opportunity for an indirect suggestion. You might notice the feelings of happiness which you have as you contemplate how good you look at your ideal weight.

8. A person might, <person's name>, _____

[Say the person's name close to the second half of the sentence, and it becomes a personal embedded command.] A person might, Sarah, take the lessons from that situation and realize how valuable it would be to experience hypnosis for yourself. A person might, Allen, find some good reasons that would make being hypnotized compelling.

9. One Could _____, because...

[Because is the magic word, because it lends emotional credibility to whatever goes before it.] Once could use the word "because" after important suggestions, because you enjoy trying new things. One could let this learning go to a very deep place inside, because you may not be completely aware of how important it is yet. One could experience hypnosis because that person was completely aware of how important it is to be smoke free. One could desire to be self-assured, because one knows how important that can be in dealing with others.

10. You can _____, because....

[Here's that because word again.] You can just use it and discover how powerful it is, because you can pretty much say anything you want after it. You can believe it works, because it is such a nice way to keep talking and keep the suggestions coming. You can even use it in everyday conversations, because people love to hear reasons for things. You can experience hypnosis, now, Stanley, because you want to be the very best you can be, don't you?

11. You can _____, can you not?

[Can you not is such a great way to end a statement. It turns the statement into a question which is less threatening, and it's so confusing to try to disagree with the statement/question.] You can appreciate my point, can you not? You can find lots of reasons for experiencing hypnosis, can you not? You can realize how happy you will be when you are totally free of the smoking habit, can you not? You can do all these things, can you not?

Chapter 3 Challenges:

Review key course concepts: SRT, MPTWs, Rapport

Use Time Loops

Look for when Time Loops are used by others

Look for and use implied trance

Try all techniques in social settings

Leverage the power of being a hypnotist. When I was making the rounds as a presenter at conferences, I paid attention to how audiences reacted to different ways of introducing myself, such as *psychologist*, or *counselor*, or *therapist*. The best reactions were always obtained when I introduced myself as a *hypnotist,* which is because of the magic and mystery talked about earlier in this chapter. So this challenge is to ask 5 strangers about hypnosis.

4 METAPHORS AND STORIES

Why are metaphors and stories so powerful? The power lies in their ability to bypass the critical factors of the mind. Always remember that people *want* to escape into trance. People want to space out. Recall from the previous chapter how I emphasized the ages-old practice of storytelling around the campfire from our hunter/gatherer past. If you go back far enough, there was no written word, so most everything was communicated by and through stories.

Metaphors are critically important to CH/NLP because they are at the very heart of our skills. Most trainers don't have a clue about metaphors or how to leverage them. To really get into a story, you have to let go of the critical factors of the mind so you can get lost in the story, to surrender to it. That's hypnosis in a nutshell! And again, people want to go into that altered state when listening to a really good story. Rapport is still absolutely key to this process.

The power of metaphors and stories totally applies to movies. Movies have to present characters that you can relate to in order for you to really get hypnotized by them. Or you have to really identify with the theme or idea of the movie.

If your goal is to be a good hypnotist, and especially if you want to be a really good conversational hypnotist, you simply must become a great storyteller. Metaphors can lead step by step into deeper layers of consciousness. One such layer would be *heightened awareness*. When you come out of a really superbly crafted scary movie, *everything* scares the living daylights out of you, right? That's because you're in a very heightened state of awareness. But it's important to note that same thing with comedy. After you see a really well-crafted comedy movie, *everything* becomes funny! This also applies to romance movies, or inspirational movies like *Rocky*. Whatever big-picture genre or theme the movie contains, if it was done well it creates a very heightened state of awareness to that theme in the target's life. It's a very powerful leverage point for you to lead your target where you want them to go.

Most good stories involve the ide of **obstacle removal**, such as in Cinderella with her stepsisters. There is some kind of obstacle standing in the way of the protagonist achieving their objective or goal or dream. So let me ask you this: *What would happen if...*

You fully understood how to easily develop a metaphor?

Y could plot out what you want the metaphor to accomplish?

You knew how to break it down?

You understood how to deliver it?

When using a metaphor or story, you can layer in other CH/NLP techniques that will really enhance the power of what you're doing. Remember, there's no big secret to any of this! Most people make metaphors much more complicated than they need to be. The concept itself is really quite simple, so keep it simple, stupid (the KISS principle)!Great stories are simple, archetypal and very basic. Good metaphors and stories have awesome therapeutic power, and sales power as well. Therapists are guilty of totally underutilizing the power of stories and metaphors. Interestingly enough, their power is also often not understood properly by either hypnotists or NLP practitioners! Some of this can be blamed on misunderstanding the *Erickson Method*.

To make proper use of the Erickson Method, you have to first have a solid understanding of basic hypnotic techniques. You have to understand true rapport, know when you have, and know how to maintain it. Whatever story or metaphor you're going to use, it has to have meaning for both yourself and your target. Erickson mixed in a lot of traditional elements into his story method. Here's a quote from author Salman Rushdie that helps explain the power of stories: "Human beings, you see, do absolutely two primary things. We see like and unlike. Like becomes, in literature, simile and metaphor. Unlike becomes uniqueness and difference, from which I believe, the novel is born."

To **learn how to do metaphors**, you have to become an avid story listener yourself. That means you have to be constantly exposing yourself to new material through books, movies, plays, music, and comedy.

MOVIES: The greatest movies of all time are very powerful stories with powerful metaphors. I'm talking here about classic movies like *Star Wars*, *It's a Wonderful Life*, and the *Wizard of Oz*. More recently, we can highlight movies such as *Frozen*, or *Dallas Buyers Club*. They are powerful because they touch a place in your heart, and they also spark the imagination.

MUSIC: Music is such a powerful and effective trance inducer. Music can also elicit powerful emotional states and responses in listeners. Think about music that makes you just want to get up and dance. And what is dance if not a very hypnotic kind of movement? Any genre of music can accomplish this according to the tastes of listeners. Music that contains lyrics can obviously also combine not only the hypnotic power of melody, but also direct storytelling through the words of the song. Think now also about how the soundtrack music of a movie can completely alter and enhance the motion picture itself. This is where you can start to really develop a soundtrack for your own life. Envision yourself really doing well at whatever it is you want to do well at, and as you're seeing that in your mind, think of a song that goes with it, without any editing or rational thought, just whatever song comes into your head. Whatever it is, that's *your* soundtrack. For me, when thinking about being really good at hypnosis, the song that became my soundtract for that is *I'll Take You There*, by the Staple Singers back in 1972. You can easily see how this song would be conducive to being good at hypnosis.

BOOKS: Books are also huge trance inducers. As a developing hypnotist, you need to stay up-to-date not only with new releases, but also with the classics. In recent times, there's *Fifty Shades of Grey* by E. L. James, which contains a powerful metaphor about hidden desires. Then there's the *Hunger Games* series by Suzanne Collins, which contain the powerful metaphor of overcoming the obstacle of the "establishment." And of course classic good books, like The Hobbit by J. R. R.

Tolkein, are often translated into powerful motion pictures as well. Every book you read, whether new or old, is new material you can leverage in your CH/NLP efforts.

Stories are powerful because the imagination has no boundaries. In a story, you can literally get away with murder. You can embed direct commands into your stories for your listening targets. There's no conscious conflict with such suggestions because the target thinks it's just a story. So when you do this, there's really no need to be covert about it at all. In fact, be blatant! You don't need to try to hide the commands or the outcomes at all. All those books, movies and music are put it all right out there without hiding anything. If anything, it's what I call *hiding in plain sight*. If you're up front with it, people actually won't notice it, even though it's right in front of them or right under their noses. But as soon as you start *trying* to hide things, people pick up on that. Obama was very blatant with his hypnotic techniques he followed many of the so-called *laws of power* quite explicitly in his speeches and presentations.

Elements of stories and metaphors: Your story has to have some kind of goal or outcome in mind for the main character(s). Then there have to be obstacles in the way of obtaining that goal. In Shakespeare's *Romeo and Juliet*, the goal for the two main characters is simply to be in love, but then serious obstacles get in the way in the form of their feuding families and society in general. The story can have both direct and indirect messages, but either way it must make use of all the senses, including the visual, auditory, kinesthetic, olfactory and gustatory (taste) senses. Keeping your story well-grounded in the senses will make it much more powerful. Then of course, the story must have some kind of climax or solution inside it.

When you engage in split consciousness during the telling of your story and the target is going into trance, you can layer in all sorts of things that you want to accomplish, which can all be tangents within the overall storyline.

There's a very conscious effort to plan and practice your story. Begin by asking yourself these two questions:

What do you want your story to do? What obstacles and other elements can you put in the story that will resonate with your target? You can work every single concept we've talked about into your stories (time loops; PTWs; language patterns; implied trance; disjointed logic, and so on).

It all starts with, "You know, that reminds me of a story..."

> At the height of the Napoleonic wars, Napoleon is separated from his troops. And of course he was somewhat scared, which was a new experience for him, because usually he was not scared. After all, why would Napoleon ever be scared? He's the emperor of Europe! He's one of the most powerful men in the world. At the time, he had the largest standing army. But to be separated from his men, and feeling vulnerable and scared, that was very new for him. Have you felt scared? That's interesting, isn't it? Especially when it's new to you. And this was a really new thing for

him to be vulnerable and scared.

So he was looking for a place to hide because he knew if the Cossacks found him they would kill him outright. He looks all over the place and just can't find a place to hide. Finally he's drawn to a store. It happens to be a furrier. Inside he sees the shop owner, who asks, "How may I help you?" Because the shop owner was really there to help him. And Napolion says, "I'm Napoleon and I'm the most powerful man in the world and I can give you things beyond your wildest dreams, but I need your help." This was hard for Napolion, because he wasn't used to asking for help. He started out with bravado, but he still had to ask for help. And that wasn't something he was used to. And that's interesting for a lot of people – asking for help or admitting not knowing or having all the answers. But there he was doing exactly that.

The shop owner tells him hide under a pile

of furs. The Cossacks come along and kick in the door and demand to know if Napoleon is there. The furrier says no. The Cossacks are looking around and poking around. The furrier is the very picture of being calm, cool, and collected even though he could be killed at any moment. He just acted like he knew what he was doing.

Now they're poking their bayonets into the piles of furs and they get to the one that Napoleon is under, but the furrier is still very calm, knowing things will work out. Cannons suddenly sound in the distance and the Cossacks run out of the shop to go and join the battle. Napoleon comes out and checks himself over for possible injuries, but the shop owner knows he won't find any. After all, he knew how the situation would go and knew it would be all right.

Finally, Napoleon's men come and they are reunited. Napoleon thanks the furrier for his help. The furrier asks, "How did it feel, being so close to death?" This offends Napoleon deeply, because shop owner is just a peasant compared to him. How dare he speak to him that way? Napoleon commands his men to take the furrier outside and execute him, and that he himself will give the command.

They take the man out and blindfold him. The troops line up for the firing squad. Napoleon gives the opening sequence of the execution – Ready! Aim! And then Napoleon comes and tears the blindfold off and says, "There, now you know how it feels to be close to death!" But the furrier just smiles, because that was his point all along; that it was the *experience* Napoleon went through that was important.

So why do I tell this story at the start of a class or training or situation where people are learning something new? A lot of people coming into a class about hypnosis or NLP or psychology are coming from a perceived position of power – and in the story, Napoleon is the power figure. But there's also a "regular" guy, the shopkeeper. But *is* he just a regular guy? Napoleon has to ask for help and give up some control, which is not easy. With people coming into the class, I try to appear like the regular guy as much as I can, without touting my credentials and all that stuff. In this version of the story, I didn't put in much sensory material, but you can and should put lots of it in there, utilizing all the senses. You can also heighten states a lot more than I did in that particular telling. The purpose of the story is about following directions, and that's what I want people to do in an introductory or basic class – take it all in, don't ask a lot of questions, and follow the instructions to get into the concrete experiences offered in the class. The commands I embed in the story are essentially *help me, do what I say, follow my instructions*. All the power material about Napoleon gets anchored to myself to embed and enhance my status as the teacher and sharer of knowledge.

It's very useful to understand the **basic mind control formula** (and I'll go more deeply into this when I talk about cults in a later chapter). The steps are as follows:

Encourage a dream

Justify failures or setbacks

Confirm their suspicions

Allay their fears

Create a common enemy or opponent

If you go back and re-read the introduction to this book, you'll find all five steps incorporated into it.

Of course, all of this depends upon rapport. You also have to be passionate about it, and that passion has to come through *in your voice* when you tell a story. Delivering any story without passion and emotion in your voice is simply a dead end. You have to elicit the desired state in yourself before you can expect anyone else to come along for the ride! I've given whole webinars about passion as the missing link in much of what we do. I've been blessed with several different passions: Hypnosis, psychology, martial arts, plays/acting. We find ourselves drawn to people who exhibit real passion because we want that passion as well.

Here's another round of hypnotic language patterns for you to practice:

12. I don't know if _____.

I don't know if you are going to like this training more than any other training you have ever experienced. I don't know if you are going to enjoy certain things in particular more than others. I don't know if you will enjoy the language patterns more than anything else. I don't know if this experience is going to change your life. I don't know if experiencing hypnosis is the most important decision you may ever make.

13. You might notice how good...feels, when you...

[The hidden assumption is that what I'm suggesting feels good, and the when you part further assumes that you are going to do it!] You might notice how good you feel when you realize what hypnosis can do for you. You might begin to notice, now, how good it feels when you write the check for your initial hypnosis session. You might notice how good your eyes feel when you close them and they stay closed.

14. One doesn't have to, <person's name>

[One doesn't really have to, does one. It seems so formal and detached and impersonal, (person's name), or does it?] One doesn't have to, Barbara, begin to imagine how much better you will look and feel when you are making better grades. One doesn't have to, Fred, realize how much better he will look and feel when he is at his ideal weight.

15. People don't have to <person's name>, _____

[People don't have to, but they do anyway, doesn't it seem like that? And when I use your name, it makes it so personal.] People don't have to respond favorably when you use their name, but you know, Stanley, they sure do. People don't have to, Marilyn, listen carefully to everything I say. People don't have to, Clarence, understand how easy it can be to be smoke free through the use of hypnosis.

16. You may not know if _____.

[When I wonder whether you know something, I presuppose that something exists and is true.] You may not know if hypnosis is going to be just right for you. You may not know if you're going to be SO happy with

hypnosis that you'll have to write me and tell me about it. You may not know if this training is going to be really fun and exciting.

17. It's easy to _____, is it not?

[Is it not is another one of those endings that softens a statement into a question. Additionally, it's somewhat confusing to disagree with, is it not?] It's easy to see what good sense it makes to experience hypnosis, is it not? It's easy to realize how much better off you'll be twenty years from now by becoming smoke free, now, is it not? It's easy to make a decision to experience hypnosis now, is it not? And, if I say something is easy, you may be willing to do it to see if I'm right.

Chapter 4 Challenges:

Watch a few movies outside your normal purview, and I mean really go out to a movie theater, because it's just not the same as watching a movie at home on your TV or computer.

Develop 3 stories for common things you come across. See an example below after the challenges. Memorize and tell your stories to people.

Practice the hypnotic language patterns.

Example story:

I did a lot of weight loss for a time in my clinical practice. People often have some early success and then hit a roadblock and stop losing or relapsing into poor eating habits. If someone lost 15 pounds, I will graphically show them what that is by having them pick up a 15-pound bucket of real lard. The point is that what they're doing is taking their accomplishment and minimizing it, whereas I want to make it big. After setting it down, I'll say, "That reminds me of a story...

> Mary was going to set out on a journey, but
> she didn't really want to set out because
> she as all closed in by her thinking. She
> didn't realize she needed to change. She
> put on all these layers because she thought
> it was going to be cold, without even
> knowing if it was really cold outside or not.
> She assumed it was cold and bleak outside
> because that's how she felt. There were so
> many layers that no one could get in, no
> one could get through to her. But finally she

reached out for help, because she was
scared. Have you eve been scared? Mary
reached out for help and did go on the
journey with her companion, shedding the
layers as she went, but then Mary came to a
wall and she was scared. But her
companion said not to be scared. She said
they should examine the wall. Upon closer
examination, it was like a wall on a movie
set, made of flimsy Styrofoam. As it turns
out, the wall was only supported by Mary's
own fears. With the help of her companion,
Mary broke through that wall, she shed her
layers and got rid of them. She was so
thankful to her companion that she had
tears in her eyes, because now she knew
she could do it. And she turned to thank the
person, and it turned out that her
companion was really her own higher self.

Now I would bring her out of the trance and give some
additional commands about sticking with the plan during
the coming week. You can also make up a whole story
about the gift of wholesome fruits and vegetables and
getting off the junk food and highly processed foods. You

can add in items about exercise as well. Simple? Yes. Effective? You bet!

5 LOGICAL LEVELS

Logical Levels are important because you can do all sorts of things with them. Understanding logical levels also serve to open up an understanding of how neurosis occurs in people. You can actually utilize logical levels to install neuroses in other people – not that you'd ever want to do that, but it is important to at least understand how it works.

What are logical levels? The self operates on a variety of layers or levels. The spirit or spiritual level is the highest, most abstract level of the self. It is the basis for the Milton Model. This is the level of the collective consciousness. The next level down is your identity level, who you are. And by that I mean who you *really* are, like when no one else is looking. The next level down from there is the belief level, what it is that you believe. This level also includes your values because they flow directly from your beliefs about the world. Next comes the level of capabilities and skills. Sometimes you need to change those. Next is a level that includes all of your behaviors. And finally there is the level of your environment, which means where you are – your house, home, friends, family, workplace. Does your environment support what it is you're trying to accomplish in your life? This came up a lot when I was doing weight loss work. Losing weight and keeping it off will be difficult if you don't also change the environment of what types of food you have in your refrigerator or pantry. If your home environment is filled with unhealthy foods, weight loss will be next to impossible.

This is important because if your environment isn't supportive of the behaviors you're trying to adopt, success will be difficult. Sometimes you can change your environment and behaviors will naturally change. Other times you're trying to engage in new behaviors but you haven't changed your environment to support that. If you're trying to quit drinking alcohol, you will be more successful if you change your environment by not going to bars!

Some people go to a hypnotist because they lack the capabilities and skills they need to really change their behaviors in the ways they want, which means a lot of the work will take place on that skill level.

The belief level is very important because if you're trying to make a change but your belief system is one that says it's going to be very difficult, that can greatly affect your chances of success. Smokers often say how difficult or hard it is to quit smoking. But is it? Lots of people do it all the time, so maybe a change of belief is in order. Beliefs will make the behavioral change either easier or more difficult than it needs to be.

Does your identity support you making the change you want to make? I was doing a smoking cessation workshop and this guy comes up to me to register for the session. He's wearing a Marlboro belt buckle, Marlboro jacket, has a pack of Marlboros in his shirt pocket, and is wearing a Marlboro Nascar baseball cap. Now you tell me, is a change of identity in order here?

Obviously, the answer is yes! Smoking is clearly a deeply embedded aspect of his identity. Change your identity so there's a clash of identity and behavior and that will facilitate the change.

The Milton Model and Ericksonian hypnosis techniques emphasize the importance of climbing up to that highest level to accomplish the most significant work of change in the individual. The key to using Logical Levels is to assess where the person is at and then work the levels that need to be worked. If a person lives very much in the esoteric realm of the spiritual level, then you might need to work on some of the lower levels to facilitate the desired change.

When you "chunk up" through the levels, you're working to bring the various levels into an alignment that all supports the desired change. The same thing occurs when "chunking down," where someone needs to come back down into the more physical aspects that need to be brought into alignment with the desired change. Chunking up tends to be working someone into trance whereas someone who's always in the higher levels and trance needs to be brought back down and more out of trance.

Here's where we can talk about advanced split consciousness, where you either take them up but focus them down or take them down and focus them up. This is a way of making a person aware of the conflict and a split occurs. Example: *The Escalator Induction*.

> Have you seen any of the Harry Potter movies? One of the interesting things about Harry Potter is that the movies and books are all about magic and how we all really believe in magic. Do you believe in magic? I believe in magic. I believe that magic really does happen. Whether it's a magician on stage performing tricks that you just can't figure out how they happen, you know it's just an illusion of magic, but I believe in real magic. That's what the Harry Potter books are all about, real magic happening, and about children believing in themselves. Remember when you were a child how you believed in magic? You can think back to your childhood and remember what it felt

like to really believe in magic. You wanted
to believe in that magic. And today
sometimes when you see a magician, you
really want to believe in that magic, right?
Because belief is everything.

In the Harry Potter books there is the
Ministry of Magic, a wonderful building
where magic and miracles are stored. If you
had your own Ministry of Magic, what
would it look like? Would it be a big castle
like in ancient times? Would it be a kind of
futuristic thing you might see in space? But
if you walked into your own Ministry of
Magic, one of the things that could happen
is there might be magical escalators right
when you walk in. And with that childlike
belief in magic, you notice that your body
gets on the down escalator while your mind
gets on the up escalator. So your body is
going to go deeper as your mind is going
higher. And as you go from level to level
your body is going deeper and deeper into
relaxation while your attention goes higher

and higher into the esoteric and spiritual, almost as if you're going to commune with God in a place of magic and miracles as your body goes deeper and deeper into relaxation. Isn't that amazing?

And so finally you'll approach that place of where all magic and miracles are stored, and that place is your higher self, your higher consciousness. From way up here you can see your body way down there, and what's interesting is that you can see some applications of these logical levels. Take addictions, for example. You can look way down there and see yourself getting those addictive substances out of your environment. Or weight loss – you can see yourself getting all those unhealthy foods out of your fridge and pantry, getting them out of your environment. And you can now add behaviors as well, perhaps you can see yourself exercising more regularly or making healthier food choices while grocery shopping. And you can see yourself taking away those behaviors that aren't helpful for the desired changes. And while you're in this wonderful place of magic and miracles, it's a great time to maybe change some beliefs about yourself that would help. It's a good time to believe that the change you want can actually happen easily and effortlessly because you believe that. So now that you're leaving your very own Ministry of Magic, keep this interesting idea of the logical levels and what you can do with them because you can do great things with them.

It is conflict between logical levels that creates neurosis. For religiously minded people, it's preaching the gospel but living in sin. It could be the homophobe who indulges in a gay relationship. Sometimes you hate something because you can't seem to control it when you want to be able to control it. This hate/indulge process is a conflict between your logical levels, oftentimes a conflict between beliefs and behaviors or behaviors and environment. Hypocrisy is a conflict of logical levels.

You have to bring those levels into alignment by changing things like identity, beliefs, behaviors, etc. That's why Christianity has this whole notion of being "born again." It's like an instant identity change to which you can align everything else. This is what 12-step programs do as well, sometimes focusing on environmental changes that will align better with the desired state. And notice how the 12-step programs are very spiritually focused as well. They're working all the levels in a very conscious way.

Embedded Commands: You can embed commands into sentences that have a powerful effect on people. It has to be strong, not a *request*, but a *command*. It has to stand out from the dialogue surrounding it in some way, whether that is louder, softer, faster, slower, whatever. In acting it's called "punching" a line to make it stand out. In the context of CH/NLP, it's called "marking" it from the rest of the dialogue. The brain always takes immediate note of something that is suddenly different, such as an embedded command delivered as a marked phrase. Example:

I know that ***you, like me***, want the field of

CH/NLP to grow and help the world as it *helps you*. I know that *by now*, you're ready to *join me* on this quest. Only *you can convince yourself that now* is the time to *help me spread the word* about this and other courses, which is why I am building a true referral network *for you*, and affiliate program *for you*. As you look towards your bright future, you can clearly see how helping me helps you.

Notice the link that happens between "you like me" and "helps you" that sets it into the mind that you liking me actually helps you. Note that "by now" can also get stuck in the mind as "buy now" if you're selling something. Then there is a clear command to convince yourself to help me spread the word now. Also notice how the referral network and affiliate program are positioned as being "for you." Finally, a bright future awaits if you help me because that is really helping yourself as well. Each embedded command must be delivered as a marked phrase.

Then you can see how you start working these

embedded commands into a logical level routine that facilitates going into trance: "As you relax and *go higher*" includes a marked phrase that facilitates chunking up through the logical levels.

Command Basics: It's still all about rapport. Remember, if you don't have rapport, your efforts will come off as condescending or manipulative and trigger your target's BS detector to go on high alert. You'll never get away with embedded commands if you don't obtain good rapport. They need to flow and be really natural.

You have to have a very clear vision in mind for what you want the target to do. As you're delivering the embedded command, you need to picture in your mind your target actually doing what you want them to do. That seems very simple, but it's totally essential and works much better that way. If you don't picture it, your energy isn't right. Picturing it makes the exchange of energy become synergistic with what you want to happen. Also be blatant. Most people don't really understand what you're doing to begin with, so there's no need to try and hide it too much.

These embedded commands work in all sorts of

situations, and especially in any kind of sales or marketing application. They are also very applicable in any kind of seduction/dating situation.

During one course I taught on this subject, the challenge was to try to get someone to change their order in a restaurant using these techniques. It is a really fun exercise to make this happen. And you can really push the envelope and see how far you can take it, so give it a try!

Here are more hypnotic language patterns for you to practice:

18. A person may not know if _____.

[For added fun a person can change the subject of the sentence halfway through. It's mildly confusing and it underlines that you aren't really talking about a person in the abstract anyway.] A person may not know if you're going to realize, now, how valuable hypnosis can be in removing unwanted stress and anxiety. A person may not know if you're going to have a meaningful experience through this training. A person may not know if you're going to have as much fun during this

training as anyone. A person may not know if anyone who experiences hypnosis will get a great deal out of it.

19. *You are able to _____.*

You are able to enjoy being in this training, because you really enjoy learning new and exciting things. You are able to understand how hypnosis provides you with the tools for change. You are able to re-read this to make sure you get it. You are able to do all of this and much more.

20. *<fact>, <fact>, <fact>, and _____.*

[When you start off saying a string of facts, the other person internally is thinking "yes," "yes," and "yes," and they get into the habit of agreeing with you. That is when you present him/her with your suggestion.]
You've made a success of yourself in the business world, you have a beautiful wife and family, it's important to be free of unnecessary stress by experiencing hypnosis, you will be able to rid yourself of unnecessary and unwanted stress. Things are more hectic in the business world every day, there is no way to avoid increased business complexities, everyone needs a way

to be protected from increased stress and hypnosis provides you with that.

21. A person is able to _____.

[What do most people do when I comment on what other people are able to do? They usually do an internal check to see if they can do it too.] A person is able to make the kinds of changes she wants, and cause them to be permanent. A person is able to recognize how disastrous it can be to fail to protect his health by becoming smoke free. A person is able to realize just how powerful is this word pattern. A person is able to understand that this word pattern is very powerful.

22. ...once told me, "_____"

[Quote someone else and put your message in the quote. The nice thing is that they said it, you didn't.] My favorite uncle once told me, "Take care of yourself when you are young and you'll have good health when you're old." My dad once told me, "A good hypnotist is worth her weight in gold." Jim Heil once told me, "Use these language patterns and you'll be able to persuade people a lot more effectively."

23. *...said, "_____"*

[The same pattern applies in this one, where you quote someone else and put your message in the quote.] Time and again people who I have trained in these language patterns have said, "Quotes are one of the slickest ways to deliver indirect messages." In fact, one of them once said, "If you can't use quotes to deliver a message, you must be brain dead!" *[Of course, that was him. That's the sort of thing I would never say.]*

Chapter 5 Challenges:

Review the content up to this point with new eyes, new ears and a new perspective.

Use Logical Levels on 3 people.

Apply Split Consciousness with levels.

Listen for Logical Levels in the news. Example: The person who owns Indianapolis Colts was stopped for Driving Under the Influence, and the police found prescription drugs in the car as well. And he also had $29,000 in cash on him. They really highlighted that last bit about the huge amount of cash. The obvious implication is that he must have been going to do something illegal with it, right? But he's worth 1.4 million, so in reality it's just chump change. What does that have to do with anything?

Use commands.

Listen for commands (obviously commercials use embedded commands all the time).

6 MAGIC POWER WORDS AND CULT METHODS

Naturally, easily, effortlessly. These are Magic Power Words.

Magic Power Words serve the purpose of softening whatever you're saying in a way that allows it to become more readily accepted by the target. In this method, you put adverbs *before* verbs and adjectives *before* nouns because it creates the presupposition that what follows is true. It's like a kind of linguistic lubricant that allows what you're saying to really slip easily and effortlessly into the mind of the target, and it's very powerful.

Words like aware (ness), realize (realizing), notice (ing),

experience (ing) discover (ing) are especially powerful because they signal the brain of the target to begin doing the thing that you are actually describing. The target will engage the mental process you're describing. It presupposes that everything that follows is true for the target. You bypass resistance by asking them if they notice or realize something. The target does have to focus enough on the process to actually do it for it to be effective.

Ever notice how effective NLP is?

Are you realizing the true power of NLP?

As you become aware of how you're sitting, you notice that you want to move.

Then, if you combine that awareness and focus with the adverb/adjective routine, you'll really see things open up for you:

Naturally as you become aware of the true power of this, you'll want to keep on learning more about it.

As you effortlessly notice yourself following along, you start to realize your true needs, and you naturally, easily and effortless want to experience more.

It really does work like magic in your target's mind. They really won't notice what you're doing. And once you get the gist of this, then you can layer in even more, such as embedded commands:

*Naturally as you become aware of those true deep needs, and you effortlessly want to experience true growth, you can **sign up now** for a personal coaching session.*

*As you effortlessly discover new ways to experience this wonderful state, you will easily find yourself **signing up for more sessions now**, right?* (Notice the "tag question" at the end of this one).

You can use these Magic Power Words in your split consciousness routines as well:

*As you effortlessly listen to me you can easily focus on your hands. As you easily notice your hands as you notice my voice, you can realize that **you are relaxing now**.*

*As you easily look at the light, you notice your **breathing***

slowing down, *don't you? That's right.*

You can also bring your time loops into alignment with Magic Power Words:

Many people easily notice that as they imagine and realize their future they can experience more joy in the here and now.

As you naturally notice how your past can color your future, you can easily imagine new learning from that old past.

Notice how sometimes when these phrases appear out of the context and atmosphere, they sound very stilted and strange, but in reality they really do work like magic. And that's the difference between writing them down and reading them as opposed to speaking them, which is the context in which we use them in CH/NLP.

This is where it's very useful to put aside your own political beliefs and listen to the brilliant campaign speeches of people like Clinton and Reagan and see how much of this appears in their speeches. And of course you can connect these Magic Power Words into your Logical Level routines as well:

As you easily and effortlessly connect with your higher self, you can notice new things in your physical body, and you can discover new ways to heal and comfort yourself without the old destructive methods of the past. (Good for addicts).

You begin to easily notice how your new identity doesn't allow you to go back to those old playgrounds. (Good for addicts).

And if you add these into your use of metaphors and storytelling, it makes those methods much more effective. It makes the story really hypnotic.

One of my personal favorites is the **More More Pattern**, which follows the structure of "the more you X the more you Y." Using this, you can link any two thoughts or ideas whether they make logical sense or not! "The more you look for reasons to resist me, the more you really just want to let go and follow my commands." Or, "The more you look for excuses to skip exercising, the more you really just want to jump in and do it now." Or, "The more you get mad at me, the more you love me." It's a powerful link that can work wonders. That's why the people who have the most passionate sex often are also the ones who love each other most deeply.

People who get to be really good at this find ways to link all of these different techniques and methods together into scripts that work really well. That's why you have to master each of the techniques separately, because the true power lies in being able to weave them all together into a truly masterful script that gets you where you want to be.

It's also useful to understand how mind control works in the cult setting. How does one build a cult following? It happens in 5 surprisingly easy steps:

1. Encourage their dreams. Unfortunately, most people's dreams are smashed to bits and taken away from them by parents, authority figures, or society in general. This is perplexing in a society where we idolize and worship success and daring, but tend to ridicule the people around us who express the desire to go for that themselves.

When I took acting classes in college (and this was after spending a couple years as an actor in Los Angeles) I noticed that the acting teachers themselves would do this. Young people would come to the classes with their dreams of becoming an actor and the teachers would inevitably try to put them on a teaching track or something practical because you have to actually make a living as well. The clear implication was that they wouldn't be able to become an actor, and the teachers were smashing those dreams. So for my senior project, rather than directing or starring in a play as most students would do, I put together this whole presentation about how to become a professional actor. I did this because I had already done it and learned the ropes, and the students weren't really getting the right information from the teachers because they were too busy smashing their dreams and being all practical about teaching acting rather than trying to do it professionally. Well, the powers that be of the college caught wind of my plans and they actually called me in and tried to dissuade from giving this seminar. Why? Because I was encouraging the students' dreams! They claimed they didn't want the students to have false hopes. The head of the theatre department was trying to get me to switch gears and go the traditional route, but I held my ground, maintaining that I had already finished the work of putting the project together. It was done. And then I pulled a real power play. I told him I would happily submit my project to the president of the university and explain how I thought it was very strange that a theatre department wouldn't give its students any practical knowledge about how to become a professional actor! I did wind up getting an A on the project, but it really highlighted to me just how often people are in the business of smashing other people's dreams rather than encouraging them. If you encourage people's dreams, you become a magnet to people because they want their dreams, right?

2. *Justify their failure.* You have to make sure people think that it's not their fault that they haven't achieved their dreams. You rationalize it based on whatever set of forces can be construed to be holding them back or keeping them down.

3. *Confirm their suspicions.* People naturally have suspicions about why they haven't achieved their dreams, suspicions that something has been holding them back. And you confirm that by building on step 2. Maybe the government has been withholding information that would have been useful. Maybe people are being manipulated by big corporations. You want to try to base this in truth as much as possible, which is easy to do because there's all kinds of compelling evidence for whatever story you're trying to create, and that does give you a nice out. And it works because none of us likes to take personal responsibility for our failure to achieve our dreams and hopes. Interestingly enough, the best leaders do take responsibility for things, but the mindset they create in their followers is that the fault does not lie with them (the followers).

4. *Allay their fears.* You allay their fears by showing yourself to be like them, and that you are there to help them. You are the one who really understands their problem, and if you have personal experience with that, all the better. If you can claim you were fat, or broke, or homeless, or whatever, that's powerful stuff. All the Internet marketers seem to have been the exact opposite of what they most recently achieved!

5. *Create or find a common opponent.* You have to find this common enemy. This may be the same source of the suspicions in step 3, but it doesn't have to be. It's just a common opponent you can vilify as being the real problem that must be stopped or resisted. Hitler used Jews. The far right wing in the US blames welfare recipients or liberals, and so on.

If you draw people in and work them through all these levels, you can basically create a cult. And if you add into these steps all the techniques and methods about CH/NLP that you've learned, then it can be a very powerful and easy route to creating a cult. You'd think people would see through this really easily, but history would say otherwise...

Here are some more hypnotic language patterns to practice:

24. If you _____, then ......

This is a cause and effect statement, and it doesn't have to make much sense. In order to verify that the *then* part is true, the person has to do the if part, which is what you want. If you *experience hypnosis* then you will *discover how easy it is to make the change you want.* If you *direct your attention to what hypnosis has done for others*, then *you'll be able to see how it can help you, too.*

25. When you _____, then .....

I say *when X, then Y*, and you have to *do* X and then *search for* Y in order to understand what I'm saying to you. Pretty trick, huh? When you *get in touch with the facts about how hypnosis can help you*, then *you will find it compelling to experience hypnosis, yourself.* Check it out!

26. Will you _____ now, or will you _____?

Will you do it now, or will you do it later. Will you *experience hypnosis now*, or will you *experience it right after I buy your lunch?* Will you *sign up for the program* now, or will you *sign up when we complete the intake form?* Will you *sign up* now, or will you *wait until I've given you my full sales pitch?*

27. I'm wondering if you'll _____, ... or not.

This *or not* ending is the greatest way to dodge resistance. If you see the other person smiling and nodding his/her head "yes", then there is no need to add the or not. Who needs it? I'm wondering if you'll *want to set a time for your first appointment right here and now.* (Pause. What, no enthusiastic agreement?) ... or not. I'm wondering if you'll *use this language pattern constantly* (Pause. What, no enthusiastic agreement?) .... or not.

28. People can, you know, _____.

I'm talking about what other people can do. I'm not talking about you! You know, that *you know* clause seems to imply in an ambiguous fashion that you knew this already. People can, you now, *find ways to pay for the hypnosis work they really need.* People can, you know, *provide for the changes that they want and need.*

29. Maybe you haven't ..., yet.

Maybe you haven't, maybe you have. Who knows? I'm just making an observation. When that yet comes along, there's a strong implication that sooner or later you're going to! Maybe you haven't decided to *experience the benefits of hypnosis*....yet. *Maybe you haven't* given consideration to how wonderful you will feel when you've reached your ideal weight ... yet. Who knows? There's still time. It's just an observation.

Chapter 6 Challenges:

Listen for Magic Power Words.

Use Magic Power Words in EVERY conversation.

Look for cult structure in real life.

Find a cult to study.

7 VISUAL SQUASH

Visual Squash is a very basic and powerful NLP technique. At it's essence, it is an anchoring technique that literally re-wires the brain. One of the many useful functions of visual squash is to bring items that in conflict with one another into harmonious alignment – such as the clash of logical levels that can result in neurosis, as was discussed in Chapter 5.

The fundamental pattern in visual squash is to take a situation that feels very much like an either/or clash in choice, sometimes also called a *polarity response*, and create a third option that opens up more possibilities, often by taking a both/and approach with the parts that appear to be in conflict. For example, If someone is feeling a real conflict between going to their place of employment and working to make a living versus doing all of the things they want to do that aren't their dead-end office job, the new part created might be one in which the person figures out how to make a living doing some of the things they love to do. You can easily see how this approach takes the either/or parts and squashes them down into a new choice that satisfies both in a both/and kind of way.

The interesting thing about visual squash is that it was a very early tool developed in the beginning days of NLP, so it is often overlooked or underestimated in terms of its true power. And it is a very powerful tool that is ignored by practitioners to their own detriment.

Visual squash can be used to combine skills learned in from different activities or contexts, which overcomes our natural inclination to not realize what parts of skills can be transferred to other areas of life and combined with other skills.

The reason it's called *visual* squash is that it leverages the senses into a powerful physical representation of the items being combined. You take the one concept or part of the context and place it in one hand, giving it a full range of sensory descriptors – what it looks, feels, tastes, smells and sounds like. You take the other part and do the same thing with the other hand. You go back and forth between the two hands, each time describing the item in the hand, but with each iteration the hands come closer together until they "squash" the two different concepts into one, which is a new creation that will have it's own new possibilities.

Once you have squashed the two different parts or concepts into one between your clasped hands, you physically bring that new item in your hands to your body, whether that be your chest/heart or your head. This physical motion literally brings the new creation or new state into your body, allowing it to spread and settle throughout yourself, to then be lived out successfully.

The great thing about visual squash is you can use it such a wide variety of situations. You could use it in a whole-person self-development kind of way, envisioning and describing who you are and who you want to be, and then squashing those together into a whole new you.

Now think about how you can combine many of the other core concepts into visual squash and you'll easily see just how powerful it can be. You might make up a whole story that plays out in the context of visual squash to get your points across to the target, and then embed all the commands and suggestions needed to get the target there right into the storyline itself. Make sure you throw in plenty of Magic Power Words and MPTWs along the way, use logical levels, engage in split consciousness and of course, maintain rapport throughout!

Here are some more hypnotic language patterns to practice:

30. *One might, you know, _____.*

[One might, and then again one might not. Who knows? You know!] One might, you know, just take the time to study what is available in the area of hypnosis and make the changes s/he wants. One might, you know, understand how to use this language pattern at just the right times.

31. You might want to _____, …now.

[This now is the trickiest part. If you slur it together with the rest of the sentence it just adds an imperative quality to that embedded command. If you pause and then say it, it becomes a powerful command all on its own.] You might want to consider whether hypnosis for weight loss or stress reduction is appropriate for you now. You might want to go ahead and experience hypnosis …now. Who knows, you might want to do just that.

32. You could _____.

[You could! Of course you could. You have free will.] You could sleep on it tonight, and call me in the morning. You could let this process of experiencing hypnosis take place without even knowing how it was happening. Huh? You could just let go and relax. Ok? OK.

33. You might _____.

[You might, and whatever you do might be even more likely after having it suggested like this.] You might want, more than anything, to make the changes you

want through hypnosis. You might discover that hypnosis is just the thing you need to make the changes you want. You might begin to recognize that this training is fun, exciting and valuable.

34. A person could, <person's name>, _____.

A person could, Clarence, realize that the benefits of hypnosis are extraordinary. A person could, Barbara, go to work tomorrow with a new outlook about the value of hypnosis. A person could, Michael, write a check for the initial hypnosis session, now. Heck, it's a free country.

35. You may _____.

You may find this training experience very valuable to you, in every way. You may get confused about what used to stop you from making hot money calls. You may like hypnosis so much that you'll want to recommend it to all of your friends and family members. You may, go ahead. I give you permission.

Chapter 7 Challenges:

Review all core concepts presented in this book,

including basics of NLP.

Practice and use Visual Squash.

15 BONUS HYPNOTIC LANGUAGE PATTERNS

You've stuck with me this far, so I'm going to share a final bonus set of 15 additional hypnotic language patterns for you to use practice and make your own.

36. One may, <person's name>, _____.

One may, Sarah, feel comfortable working with a hypnotist. One may, Jerry, forgive someone, even though you don't think you wanted to do so. One may, Jane, be excused from listening to more of a sales pitch after she has committed to experiencing hypnosis.

37. A person may _____, because...

A person may get permission to do what I'm suggesting,

because I'm giving it to him/her. *[Who said my because had to make any logical sense? And besides, the because clause is an opportunity for another suggestion.]* A person may go ahead and experience hypnosis, because he realizes just how much it can help him to make changes that he wants to make.

38. You don't have to _____.

[This is called a truism. The statement cannot be argued with because on the surface, it is true. Beneath the surface lies an embedded command.] You don't have to experience hypnosis today. You don't have to understand how hypnosis works to be benefited by it. You don't have to help me with the dishes. Really.

39. Will you..., or..., or...

[This is the form of infinite choice, and I'll cover all of the possibilities so you can't help but do what I say. And if you get into the habit of doing what I say, sometime I may begin to actually lead/influence you.] Will you experience hypnosis this week, or will you do it right after the first of the year, or will you create a plan for using hypnosis to help you make the changes you want?

So many choices, so little time.

40. I wouldn't tell you to _____, because...

[I wouldn't tell you (here I am telling you anyway), and you can't disagree with me, because I said up front I wouldn't tell you. And, again, I use the magic word because to make another comment, because it lends authority to what I just said, and it carries attention away from the embedded command before you consciously recognize it.] I wouldn't tell you to use this language pattern when you are trying to persuade someone to experience hypnosis, because you might feel it is so powerful that it would be unfair to use it. I wouldn't tell you to use this language pattern with your customers, clients and prospects, because it might allow you to be more influential with them than me.

41. How would it feel if you...?

[In order to answer this question, you have to imagine what I propose, which is the whole purpose for asking the question.] How would it feel if you just went ahead and experienced hypnosis? How would it feel if you discovered that hypnosis is a wonderful way for you to

make the changes you want, now?

42. I could tell you that... but...

[I could tell you that...but I won't so you have no reason to resist or to take offense at whatever I just didn't tell you.] I could tell you that this training will give you more confidence and self-assurance, but I would rather let you discover that for yourself. I could tell you that this language pattern is a great way to avoid resistance, but you probably understand that already. I could tell you that hypnosis is the perfect thing to help you become smoke free, but you probably realize that already.

43. Sooner or later...

Sooner or later you'll realize that hypnosis is the easy way to get what you want. Sooner or later everyone finds out that experiencing hypnosis provides untold benefits in the long run. Sooner or later you will find yourself using this language pattern. Jeepers, everything happens sooner or later.

44. Sometime...

Sometime, somewhere, there will be a person in a situation very much like yours, who will take a deep breath and go ahead and get the help s/he wants and needs through hypnosis. Sometime you will see a person who knows a good thing when he sees it and he will just go ahead and experience the hypnosis. Sometime you might indirectly influence a person to go ahead and experience hypnosis.

45. Eventually...

Eventually, everything comes to pass. Eventually, what I want to direct your attention to will probably come to pass as well. Eventually, you will discover how valuable the right hypnotist can help you obtain the outcome you want and you will go ahead and experience hypnosis.

46. Try to resist...

[Try to resist implies that you will try, but you won't be able to do it. You can use your voice inflection to strengthen this implication.] Try to resist the realization that when you are without the help that you need, it is impossible to make the changes you want. Try to resist

knowing that daily, all over the country, in big cities and small towns, people just like you are receiving help through hypnosis with the changes they want to make.

47. *You might not have noticed...*

You might not have noticed how often you direct other people's awareness while you are talking to them. You might not have noticed how easy it is to experience the benefits of hypnosis. You might not have noticed that hypnosis offers you an effective method for you to get what you want. You might not have noticed that thousands of Americans are experiencing the benefits of hypnosis daily. You might not have noticed a lot of things, which I, as a hypnotist, am glad to point out to you.

48. *Some people...*

[Who are those some people? The first thing a person does is to check inside to discover if s/he is one of those people. So, give people something for which you want them to check.] Some people get a strong feeling of comfort just knowing they have the benefits of hypnosis immediately available to them. Some people have a

way of finding the money that is needed for really important things.

49. I'm wondering if you'll _____ ... or not.

[Deliver the embedded command, and time the or not ending to arrive when resistance appears in the other person. You'll be agreeing with them and dispelling their resistance at the very moment their resistance appears.] I'm wondering if you'll want to tell every last one of your friends about the benefits of hypnosis ... or not. *[Of course, the effect of the embedded command remains even though you've agreed with the person's resistance.]*

50. What happens when you _____?

[In order to answer this question you must imagine what I am suggesting, which is the reason I ask. Remember, in the area of emotions and feelings, people learn just as well by vividly imagining experiences as by physically having them.] What happens when you just decide that you're going to get the changes you want through hypnosis? What happens when you consider the prospect of not having to worry about getting the

changes you want?

You can easily see from the 50 different hypnotic language patterns I've shared with you throughout this book that they are a powerful way to effortlessly increase your effectiveness at CH/NLP. Enjoy!

CONCLUSION

I want to close this book by first of all thanking you for joining me on this journey through some of the basic ideas, concepts, skills, techniques and methods of CH/NLP. My goal with this book was to show you how easy and natural CH/NLP really is, and also how powerful it can be to help you get people to where you want them to be.

These concepts and skills, if practiced frequently, rooted in real-world examples and constantly enhanced through exposing yourself to new material for stories and metaphors through books, music, plays and so on, can easily lead you to a whole new level of happiness in your own life.

I also want you to realize that this book has really only scratched the surface of the possibilities offered by CH/NLP. Like the iceberg concept introduced early on in the book, what you've read about here is at best about 10% of the whole picture.

The good news is that you can choose to start exploring the other 90% of what CH/NLP has to offer any time you want. And there's no time like the present. Please visit my website, http://www.secretmindcontrol.com to get started today! You'll be glad you did.